INKLE LOOM WEAVING

Frances B. Smith

LITTLE CRAFT BOOK SERIES

 STERLING PUBLISHING CO., INC. NEW YORK

Oak Tree Press Co., Ltd. London & Sydney

Little Craft Book Series

Aluminum and Copper Tooling
Animating Films without a Camera
Appliqué and Reverse Appliqué
Balsa Wood Modelling
Bargello Stitchery
Beads Plus Macramé
Beauty Recipes from Natural Foods
Big-Knot Macramé
Candle-Making
Ceramics by Slab
Corn-Husk Crafts
Corrugated Carton Crafting
Costumes from Crepe Paper
Crafting with Nature's Materials
Creating from Remnants
Creating Silver Jewelry with Beads
Creating with Beads
Creating with Flexible Foam
Creating with Sheet Plastic
Creative Lace-Making with Thread and Yarn

Cross Stitchery
Decoupage—Simple and Sophisticated
Embossing of Metal (Repoussage)
Felt Crafting
Finger Weaving: Indian Braiding
Flower Pressing
Folding Table Napkins
Greeting Cards You Can Make
Hooked and Knotted Rugs
Horseshoe-Nail Crafting
Ideas for Collage
Junk Sculpture
Lacquer and Crackle
Leathercrafting
Macramé
Making Paper Flowers
Making Picture Frames
Making Shell Flowers
Masks
Metal and Wire Sculpture

Model Boat Building
Monster Masks
Nail Sculpture
Needlepoint Simplified
Net-Making and Knotting
Off-Loom Weaving
Patchwork and Other Quilting
Pictures without a Camera
Pin Pictures with Wire & Thread
Puppet-Making
Repoussage
Scissorscraft
Scrimshaw
Sewing without a Pattern
Starting with Stained Glass
String Designs
String Things You Can Create
Tissue Paper Creations
Tole Painting
Whittling and Wood Carving

Dedicated to Aaron and those yet to be born.

Diagrams and photographs by Gordon R. Smith, except photographs of the shoulder bag, guitar strap and headband, which were taken by Frank Lusk.

Black-and-white photographic prints by Larry Schroth.

Contents

Before You Begin

The word "inkle" is of Scottish origin and refers to narrow woven bands or tapes. People have been weaving them for centuries. In early times, narrow strips of woven material were used as belts, headbands, bag handles or to tie and support loads. People soon learned that they could sew the strips together to create bags for gathering and carrying as well as to make items of clothing. They also satisfied their esthetic sense by brightening other woven garments with decorative inkle bands.

Woven belts often have preserved ancient traditional designs. An amazing remnant of an inkle-type woven band appeared in the exhibition of archeological finds of the People's Republic of China. This piece of a woven girdle was made in the first century A.D. during the Han Dynasty! Take a look at the front cover for a modern adaptation of this ancient work.

No single area of the world can claim to have originated inkle weaving, for it appears with myriad variations wherever textile arts have developed. It is still done by natives in such diverse places as Tibet, Madagascar, the Philippines, Lapland, South America and the southwestern United States.

Some forerunners of the inkle loom have been as simple as a group of pegs driven into the ground or even just a forked stick. The back-strap loom, used by North and South American Indians, is related to the inkle loom as well. This currently popular loom is easy to make with ice-cream

Illus. 1. A home-made wooden inkle loom and a wooden shuttle.

sticks or tongue depressors. The Colonial American lap loom is of similar design and was probably brought from Scotland, England or Scandinavia by the early settlers.

Weaving, as you may already know, is the interlacing of two sets of threads, which are at right angles, to form a web or fabric. The parallel, longitudinal threads form the warp and the crosswise threads which run perpendicular to the selvage are the weft. When you use a loom you raise half of the warp so you can place the weft thread through the shed (the space you create by separating the warp threads). Then you raise the alternate half of the warp, thus interlacing the warp and weft. Depending on what kind of loom you use, you separate the warp by threading it through heddles, wires, slats or strings with holes in the middle. In some looms, the heddles move up or down to separate the warp. In others the heddles remain stationary while the warp moves up and down (one half at a time) to create the shed. This type of loom is called a fixed heddle loom and is the basic structure of all inkle looms.

Inkle weaving—weaving narrow bands—is an excellent introduction to the craft of weaving. It is easy to learn and enjoyable to craftspeople of all ages. The equipment you need is simple, inexpensive and easy to store. It is convenient because the loom is small enough to carry around. You can inkle weave indoors or out, at home or while travelling by car, train or boat.

Because it is so versatile, inkle weaving has been taken up at camps and schools where it is a satisfying craft and hospitals have used it in occupational therapy. It is a perfect rainy day pastime, invaluable for bed-bound patients, and —best of all—it is encouraging work that progresses rapidly. You can easily weave a belt in one day!

Inkle weaving also offers a wide range of pattern and color possibilities, allowing your creative imagination plenty of room for expression. Its uses in both decorative and functional ways are endless, so inkle weaving is a challenge for both experienced and inexperienced weavers.

Equipment and Materials

First you need an inkle loom. Regardless of the particular shape an inkle loom takes, it must have the following features. You need a sturdy enough frame to hold a continuous warp under tension, with some means to adjust the tension. An inkle weave is a warp-faced weave (only the warp shows; the weft is completely covered except at the selvage), and there is considerable tightening or take-up of the warp as the weaving progresses. Finally, your loom must have a simple way of making two sheds.

You can buy one inexpensively (see the list of suppliers on page 47), or you can make one for much less with hand or power tools. You will see several different styles of inkle looms in the illustrations in this book. The most basic type is sufficient for the suggested projects. Fully illustrated directions for constructing a loom are given in Illus. 2.

You also need a flat shuttle of some sort to carry the weft through the shed. You can either purchase or improvise one by notching a paint paddle on each end to provide space to hold the weft. You can also cut a shuttle from a sturdy piece of cardboard. The edge of the shuttle must be hard and thin since you use it as a beater to press the weft tightly into place against the forming fabric.

Another alternative to a shuttle is to wrap a length of the weft round your thumb and little finger to form a figure eight. This is called a butterfly. You pass it through the shed and unwind it as you weave. You can then use the edge of a table knife to beat the weft closely into place.

You can use a wide range of yarns for inkle weaving. Many people select 2- and 3-ply weaving worsteds with a tight twist. The bright, clear colors make handsome inkle bands. Avoid any materials that are stretchy, knubby or very hairy.

They create problems when you are making the shed and separating the warp. Be sure the yarn is strong enough to hold up under the tension which you apply as you weave.

Mercerized cotton and linen are excellent inkle choices, because they are smooth and strong. Belts woven with these materials have a flatter, smoother finish than those woven with wool. Nylon and rayon are also satisfactory.

String heddles come with your loom if you purchase one. You can make them yourself out of any thin, strong, smooth yarn such as linen, cotton or nylon.

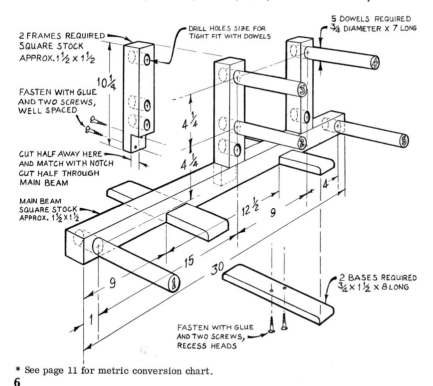

2 FRAMES REQUIRED
SQUARE STOCK
APPROX. 1½ X 1½

DRILL HOLES SIZE FOR
TIGHT FIT WITH DOWELS

5 DOWELS REQUIRED
¾ DIAMETER X 7 LONG

10¼

FASTEN WITH GLUE
AND TWO SCREWS,
WELL SPACED

4¼

4¼

CUT HALF AWAY HERE
AND MATCH WITH NOTCH
CUT HALF THROUGH
MAIN BEAM

4

MAIN BEAM
SQUARE STOCK
APPROX. 1½ X 1½

12½   9

15

30

9

1

2 BASES REQUIRED
¾ X 1½ X 8 LONG

FASTEN WITH GLUE
AND TWO SCREWS,
RECESS HEADS

Illus. 2. Pattern for an open-sided inkle loom. This type of inkle loom is easier and quicker to warp than a closed-sided loom. You can use high-grade pine for your inkle loom, but a hard wood—such as maple, walnut, oak or birch—is stronger and more attractive. Since the warp puts a fair amount of strain on the loom, you should make the joints very secure. With this particular loom, you can weave about a 5-foot* length. Other looms with sophisticated tensioning devices and additional dowels provide for a woven warp up to 8 feet long.

* See page 11 for metric conversion chart.

Belt

Materials

    inkle loom and shuttle

    $\frac{3}{4}$-inch $\times$ 5-inch wood block

    7 yards of 10/2 linen or other strong, smooth string for heddles

    2 ounces* of 2-ply rya yarn in four colors (equal amounts of teal, lime, gold and turquoise were used for the belt in Illus. 13)

    Shirt cardboard: two $\frac{1}{2}$-inch $\times$ 3-inch strips

                     one $6\frac{3}{4}$-inch-wide strip (to use as a gauge)

                     one $2\frac{1}{2}$-inch-wide strip (to use as a gauge)

Try making a simple woven belt like the one shown in Illus. 13 as your beginning project. Instructions for operating an inkle loom are the same whether you are making a basic belt or a more complicated project, so you can refer to these directions as you progress. The instructions that follow are for the hand-made inkle loom shown in Illus. 2.

Warping

You achieve the warping, tensioning and threading of the inkle loom in a single procedure. You pass half of the warp threads through heddles (loops of string) at dowel #2, while the alternate warp threads are in the open (not in a heddle). These two warping paths are shown in Illus. 3.

Before you begin warping, you have to make the heddles you need. Make 15 heddles by tying 16-inch lengths of linen yarn, one at a time, round

* See page 14 for metric conversion table of weights.

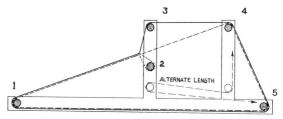

Illus. 3. The solid line illustrates the heddle warp path while the broken line shows the open warp path. Alternate these two paths when you warp the loom.

a cardboard gauge that is $6\frac{3}{4}$ inches wide. (You will be able to use these loops as heddles in all further projects in this book.) Place the wooden block on top of the rear base piece of the loom and secure it with a rubber band (see Illus. 4). (Manufactured looms have more sophisticated tensioning devices than this block.) Later, you can remove this block to slacken tension on the warp.

Now, take the ball of teal yarn (or whatever color you choose) and drape the end over dowel

Illus. 4. Place a wooden block under the base piece of the loom to serve as a tensioning device.

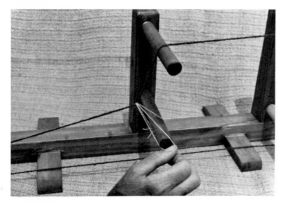

Illus. 5. Slip the heddle loop over the free end of dowel #2, as shown.

#1 at the front of the loom and then pass it over dowel #3. Set the ball of yarn down while you lay a heddle loop over the warp several inches in front of dowel #3 and slip each end of the heddle over the free end of dowel #2 (see Illus. 5). Pick up the ball of yarn and continue over dowel #4, around and under dowel #5 and back under dowel #1. This is the first heddle warp path.

Using the same teal yarn, proceed through the open warp path by passing the yarn from dowel #1 directly over dowel #4, then around and under dowel #5 and back under dowel #1.

Continue to alternate these two warping paths, as shown in Illus. 3, to form the entire warp. Be sure to maintain an even tension on all the threads as you warp them. The tension should not be very loose or very tight but somewhere in-between. Experience in warping and weaving will help you determine this. You may test the tension by gently bouncing the flat of your fingers across the

warp threads to detect loose threads. Re-tie any you find at a uniform tension.

Pattern

You create the pattern in inkle weaving by the order you place the warp threads of various colors on the loom. The weft is entirely hidden except where it wraps around the warp thread at the edge of the piece. For this reason, it is a good idea to use the same color weft as the selvage or edge warp. You might want to use a contrasting weft occasionally for special effects.

The threading chart or draft for the belt in Illus. 13 appears in Illus. 6. Read the draft from left to right alternating between the bottom and top rows representing the heddle and open warp threads. You have already warped the first two threads, so continue with the third, a heddle warp of lime. Everytime you change colors, tie the

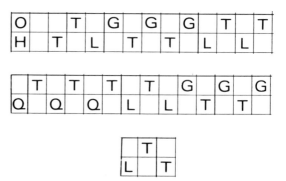

O		T	G	G	G	T	T
H	T	L	T	T	L	L	

	T	T	T	T	G	G	G
Q	Q	Q	L	L	T	T	

	T	
L	T	

Illus. 6. Threading draft for the belt in Illus. 13. Key: T = teal, L = lime, G = gold, Q = turquoise. H = heddle, O = open warp

end of the last thread you have warped (teal) to the beginning of that warp thread (teal) at dowel #1, and be sure to check the tension. In this way, you tie each individual color to itself whether you warp it once round the loom or many times.

Never tie the warp threads to a dowel, but form a loop that you can slip around the loom as the weaving progresses.

Continue warping until you have as many warp threads (29) as indicated in Illus. 6.

Weaving

Step 1: To begin weaving, place the loom on a table or chair with the front (dowel #1) towards you. Wind the yarn that you plan to use as the weft (teal if you are using the colors used here) onto the shuttle. The shuttle holds anywhere from 8 to 12 yards depending on the weight of the yarn.

As in all weaving, you must form a shed. First, depress the open warp threads just behind the heddles by placing the flat of your fingers on these threads and pressing down (see Illus. 7). Insert a $\frac{1}{2}$-inch × 3-inch strip of cardboard into the opening you just created (the shed), and slide it back close to dowel #1.

With the flat of your fingers, now lift all the open warp threads behind the heddles (see Illus. 8). This creates the alternate shed. Insert a second cardboard strip and press it tightly towards the first one. These cardboard strips serve to anchor your first weft threads in place as you begin weaving.

Depress the open warp with your fingers again and pass the shuttle through the shed from right to

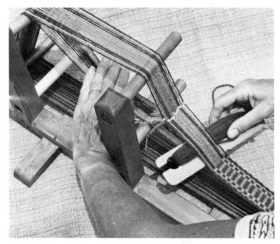

Illus. 7. Form a shed by depressing the open warp threads just behind the heddles.

left. Leave about 2 inches of the end of the weft extending beyond the warp edge, wrap the weft end around the last warp thread (selvage) and lay it

Illus. 8. To create the alternate shed, lift the open warp threads behind the shuttles.

Illus. 9. When the shed becomes too small to lift, as the web nears the heddles, slip the warp around the loom towards you, as shown.

beside the weft that you have just passed through the shed. This is the way you always secure the beginning and end weft threads.

Step 2: Lay the shuttle down on the left while you change the shed. Again, lift the open warp and lay the shuttle in the shed from left to right and pull it back towards yourself, beating the first weft thread firmly towards dowel #1 with the shuttle. You may brace the loom by placing your free hand on dowel #3. Pass the shuttle through to the right, adjust the tension of the weft in the shed so that it pulls slightly against the edge warp threads. Experience will help you know how tight to draw the weft to make an even and firm selvage. You may want to keep your first woven belt for your old pair of blue jeans, but your second you can surely sport anywhere!

Repeat these two steps to weave the entire project. The first weft shots (one passage of yarn through a shed) should draw the warp together so that the weft does not show between them. The width across the warp should be about $2\frac{1}{2}$ inches for this belt, though this may vary depending on the weight of yarn used. Whatever the width, it should remain uniform throughout the project. Use the cardboard gauge cut to the width of your woven piece ($2\frac{1}{2}$ inches) to check your work as you progress.

The first few weft shots may be a bit uneven, but you can always pull these out when you remove the belt from the loom. You must take care to beat the weft uniformly, for as the web or fabric builds up, the evenness of the pattern that develops is affected.

Moving the Warp

When the shed becomes too small, as the web nears the heddles, slip the entire warp around the loom towards you, as shown in Illus. 9. The area you have woven should slide over and under dowel #1. Remove the wooden block to release the tension and thus ease this movement. Slide the string heddles back in place as they tend to pull forward with the warp. Continue to slip the warp around the loom until the last few shots you have woven are about 2 inches from dowel #1. Re-tension the warp with the block back in place and resume weaving.

You may have to release the tension altogether as your weaving progresses, for with a warp-faced weave, a fair amount of warp take-up or tightening occurs. When you leave your loom for any length of time, release the tension so as not to leave a strain on the warp or on the dowels of the loom.

Re-filling the Shuttle

When you run out of weft on your shuttle, secure the end of the weft by wrapping it round the selvage warp and laying it in the same shed as the last weft shot. Change sheds and beat. Re-wind the shuttle and insert it in the shed opposite from the side where you just finished. Secure the end of the weft in the same manner. The ends may protrude through the warp so that you can draw the weft firm to form an even selvage. When you have completed the project, you may trim these ends close to the web so they are not visible.

Finishing

Continue weaving until the knotted ends of the warp have moved over dowel #4 and are close to dowel #3. At this point, it is difficult to make a shed. Cut the heddle warp close to dowel #3. Do not cut the heddles, as you can use them again. Cut the open warp below dowel #3. Remove the band and trim the fringe even at both ends. You may unweave the first few shots of weft if they appear loose or if the warp was not uniformly narrowed by them.

The beginning and end weft threads may hang down and be incorporated into the fringe. The web does not tend to fray, particularly when you use wool yarn, so no further finishing is necessary. Cotton or linen is slicker and might pull out, so if you used these, you might want to whip across the last few weft shots with sewing thread of a matching color to keep them in place.

Your belt is now ready to wear. Illus. 13 shows the finished belt in color.

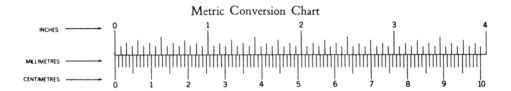

Metric Conversion Chart

INCHES

MILLIMETRES

CENTIMETRES

Designing an Inkle Band

Since the order in which you place the individual warp threads on the inkle loom determines the pattern of the band you weave, you must plan your pattern before you begin to warp the loom. Remember that the weft is only seen as it wraps around the edge and does not contribute to the design.

Plain graph paper with rather large squares is convenient for making your draft, the graphic portrayal of your design. Use only two rows of squares. These horizontal rows represent the two sheds which you create as you weave. Each square stands for a warp thread or warp end, as it is called. The bottom row depicts all the warp ends that you put through the heddles as you place the warp on the loom. Write the letter H at the far left of this row to indicate this. The top row shows all the warp that you place on the loom in the open spaces between the heddles. Write the letter O at the left of that row. Develop and read the draft from left to right.

You can vary your designs and the effects you get by experimenting with the arrangement and grouping of warp ends. Try new color combinations and different materials to add variety and lend distinction to your work. The width of the inkle depends on the number of warp ends used and the size of the yarn. For example, a 2-inch belt woven of a medium 2-ply rya yarn requires about 40 threads, while a belt made of size 3 cotton perle would need about 60. As you experiment with each material, you will learn to gauge this.

By placing light and dark colors next to one another, you can create dramatic effects. Bright colors lend a gay, folk-craft touch. Closely related colors result in a subtle, quiet pattern. Try using black and white along with other colors to create interesting effects. To achieve a balanced pattern, you might use a design in the middle of the band that is wider than the border. Inkles do not need to be symmetrical, so give your imagination free rein!

Here are a number of basic drafts. You may combine them in countless ways to form your own designs. As you use them, you may have to add or subtract a background thread to maintain the pattern on the shed you desire.

1. *Dash:* One pattern thread set in a group of background threads. See number 1 in Illus. 10.

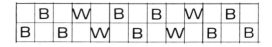

2. *Narrow line:* Two pattern threads set in a grouping of background threads. See number 2 in Illus. 10.

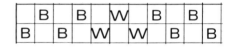

3. *Chain:* Three pattern threads among background threads. See number 3 in Illus. 10.

4. *Stripe:* Four or more threads grouped together with no background necessary. See number 4 in Illus. 11.

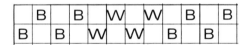

5. *Horizontal stripes or bars:* One color of threads warped through heddles and another color through the open area. (You can tie each warp thread singly or carry a small ball of each color around the loom and set it down at each color change.) The bar effect results when a fewer number of threads compose this grouping. See number 5 in Illus. 10.

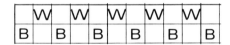

6. *Alternating bars:* Two background threads separate bars. See number 6 in Illus. 10.

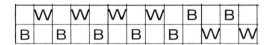

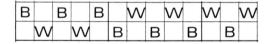

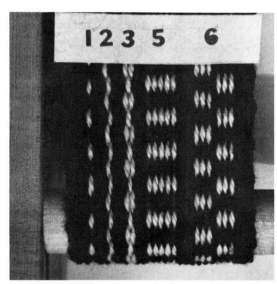

Illus. 10. Examples of various basic inkle patterns you can weave.

Illus. 11. Examples of additional basic patterns you can create.

7. *Ladder:* Stripes run along both sides of a bar. See number 7 in Illus. 11.

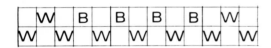

8. *Serrations:* A stripe of an odd number of threads flanked by bars. See number 8 in Illus. 11.

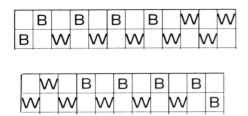

9. *Alternating serrations:* Bars flank a stripe of an even number of threads. See number 9 in Illus. 11.

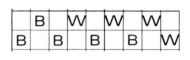

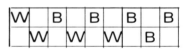

10. *Flower:* Two pattern threads against a background on one row (heddle or open) and two pattern threads separated by one background thread on the alternate row. You can heighten the effect if you use pattern threads which are of a heavier weight yarn than the background, so that they stand out in relief. See number 10 in Illus. 11.

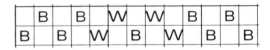

APPROXIMATE METRIC EQUIVALENTS OF U.S. WEIGHTS

| 1 American ounce | = 1 British ounce | = 28 grams (g.) |
| 1 American pound | = 1 British pound | = 450 grams |

$3\frac{1}{2}$ ounces	=	100 grams	11 ounces	=	300 grams
7 ounces	=	200 grams	12 ounces	=	350 grams
9 ounces	=	250 grams	14 ounces	=	400 grams

Shoulder Bag

Materials
  inkle loom and shuttle
  29 heddles
  $4\frac{1}{2}$ ounces of 2-ply rya yarn (approximately
    equal amounts of four colors; teal, lime, gold
    and turquoise were used for the bag in Illus.
    14)
  6-inch strip of Velcro (optional)
  $\frac{1}{3}$ yard of broadcloth (optional for lining)
  needle and sewing thread

To make a shoulder bag, you need to weave two inkle bands that you can cut and sew together. The bag pictured in Illus. 14 was designed to match the belt in Illus. 13. Begin by weaving a band in exactly the same way you wove the belt. You need a 52-inch length. Machine stitch across both ends of the band. Trim the excess warp or woven area. This piece is your shoulder strap.

Now, weave a wider band following the threading draft in Illus. 12. You will find, as you weave a wider band, that it is slightly more difficult to separate the warp and make the shed, particularly if you are weaving with wool which tends to cling or stick. It helps if you lift or depress (depending on the shed) a section of the warp at a time, working your way across the width of the band.

Weave a 57-inch-long piece. Cut this inkle into three pieces, each a total of $18\frac{3}{4}$ inches long. (See page 46 for suggestions on how to use remnants of inkles.) Machine stitch across one end of each of the bands and fray or trim, whichever is necessary, the other ends so each has a $1\frac{1}{2}$-inch fringe.

With a double strand of matching sewing thread, sew these three wide inkle bands together at their selvage, lining up the machine-stitched edges. Fold this piece as shown in Illus. 15. With the same thread, sew the edge and end of the shoulder strap to each side and the bottom of the

O		T	T	T	T	L	L	L	L	T	G	Q	Q	Q	Q
H	T	T	L	L	L	L	L	T	T	T	G	Q	Q	G	G

	Q	Q	Q	Q	G	T	L	L	L	L	T	T	T	T
G	G	G	Q	Q	G	T	T	T	L	L	L	L	T	T

Illus. 12. Threading draft for the shoulder bag in Illus. 14. Key: T = teal, L = lime, G = gold, Q = turquoise.

Illus. 13 (left). A colorful belt like the the one shown here is a simple inkle project you can make to familiarize yourself with the basic inkle techniques.

Illus. 14 (right). The shoulder bag pictured here was made to match the belt in Illus. 13. Choose colors you like to make a handsome, co-ordinated set.

bag, forming the gusset or side panel of the bag (see Illus. 16).

Lining

You may make a lining for the bag to add strength and body if you wish. Cut one piece of broadcloth 10 inches × $14\frac{1}{2}$ inches and two strips 7 inches × $2\frac{1}{2}$ inches for the gussets. Fold the large piece in half and, using $\frac{1}{2}$-inch seams, machine stitch these three pieces together, fitting the gusset strips to the edges of the folded piece. Turn under a $\frac{1}{2}$-inch hem around the top and press. Turn the lining inside out, insert it in the woven bag and slip stitch the lining to the inside of the bag. You may want to sew a short piece of Velcro on the underside of the flap and on the outside of the bag front to secure the closing.

Illus. 15. To make the shoulder bag, sew the three wide inkles together and fold as shown.

For a larger bag, you need to weave two wide inkle bands which gives you more material to work with as you sew longer strips together.

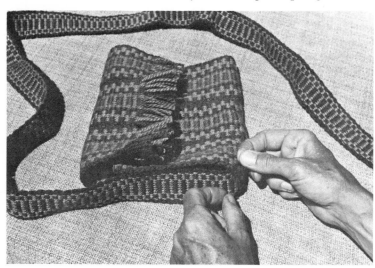

Illus. 16. Sew the narrow inkle to the bag along the sides, beginning as shown, to form the side panels and shoulder strap.

Vest

Materials
- inkle loom and shuttle
- 42 heddles
- 2-ply rya yarn (4 ounces each of navy and aqua; 2 ounces each of grey, yellow, medium green and orange were used for the vest in Illus. 21)
- needle and sewing thread

Inkle bands are often used for clothing in spite of their limited width. You can easily sew both narrow and wide bands together to fashion ponchos, skirts, stoles, bodices and vests.

The vest in Illus. 21 was made from three bands 4 inches × 60 inches and one narrow band 1½ inches × 51 inches.

Warp the loom according to the draft in Illus. 17 for the 4-inch band. Weave three. Of course,

you can design your own inkle and you vary the width of the bands to fit body measurements. Measure the distance from shoulder to shoulder to determine the width of the finished vest. The vest made following these instructions fits an average woman with shoulder measurements between 15 and 16 inches.

Next, design and weave a narrow (1½-inch) band or use the pattern suggested in the draft shown in Illus. 18.

Cut one of the 4-inch bands into two pieces, each 29 inches long. Machine stitch across one end of each piece or carefully whip across the end by hand. Fringe the other end of each piece to match the length of the fringe of the first pieces. Sew these two back pieces together, butting the sides and using a thread matching the selvage yarns.

Sew one of the remaining 4-inch pieces, which will be a side piece, to this back section, matching the fringe length. Then sew the other side piece to the other back section (see Illus. 19).

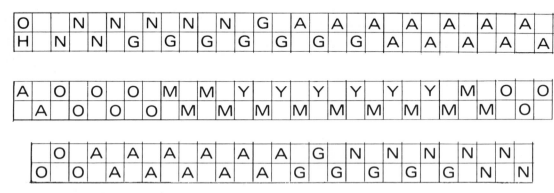

Illus. 17. Threading draft for the 4-inch band on the vest in Illus. 21. Key: N = navy, G = grey, A = aqua, O = orange, M = medium green, Y = yellow.

18

O		N		N		N		O		A		A		A		A		A		A		A		O		N	
H		N		N		N		O		A		A		A		A		A		A		A		O		N		N

Illus. 18. Threading draft for the 1½-inch band on the vest in Illus. 21. Key: N = navy, O = orange, A = aqua.

The narrow inkle forms a trim round the front and neck edge of the vest. Pin it to the front edge of the vest and across the back of the neck (see Illus. 20). Sew it in place. Make a tuck in the narrow inkle strip at the corner of the shoulder. You can stitch this on the machine and press it flat with a damp cloth.

Tie the sides of the vest together front to back with 9-inch lengths of twists of yarn. Make these twists by taking three, four or more strands of yarn (depending on the desired thickness) that are at least three times the finished length of twist you

Illus. 19. Sew a 4-inch band on each side of the back section to form the side pieces of the vest.

Illus. 20. Pin and then sew the narrow inkle to the front edges of the vest and across the back of the neck.

want. Tie the ends of these strands together and then tie them to a door knob. Back away from the door until the strands are taut. Twist the strands until they start to kink.

Double the end you are holding back on itself to meet the ends tied to the door knob while still keeping the strands under tension. Untie the ends from the door knob and, with a whipping motion, snap the strands in mid-air. They will twist into a neat cord that you can now knot at the end to preserve the twist.

For the vest ties, make a 72-inch length of twist. Cut this into eight pieces, carefully knotting one end and sewing the other end of each to prevent ravelling. Sew these pieces of twist to the sides of the vest, two above and two below the waist on each side. Tie these to fit when you wear the vest.

Illus. 21. All you need to make this stylish vest are three wide inkles and one narrow one.

Illus. 22 (right). If you have a left-over piece of inkle, or just feel like making a fairly short woven piece, why not use it to form a colorful headband, like the one pictured here.

Illus. 23. Here is an example of an attractive inkle band that you can weave. Use a decorative band like this one to create one of the projects in this book—or any other item that you think of yourself.

Illus. 24. Sometimes, you might feel like weaving an inkle band, but you do not plan ahead what to make with it. You can use such inkles, like the ones pictured here, to make anything—some unusual ideas include straps for a director's chair, a wall hanging, a mobile, an unusual room divider, curtain tie-backs, or a watch-band.

Illus. 25. By trimming an otherwise ordinary desk blotter and pencil cup with hand-made inkles, you can liven up any den or office. Directions for this desk set begin on the next page.

Desk Set

Materials
  inkle loom and shuttle
  64 heddles
  2½ ounces of 10/2 linen (equal amounts of medium blue, white, olive, grey and coral were used for the set in Illus. 25)
  blotter holder
  small (15½ ounce) tin can to use as a pencil cup
  small jar model enamel (matching or contrasting color)
  1 piece of poster board
  white, liquid glue
  small paint brush
  masking tape

A most attractive gift that is easy to make is a desk set trimmed with inkle bands. You may have a used blotter holder that you can rejuvenate or you can purchase an inexpensive one. Linen or cotton are particularly suitable for this project, as they make a smooth, flat inkle that covers the blotter panels nicely.

Using the threading draft shown in Illus. 26, or one of your own design, warp and weave an inkle 60 inches long and 3 inches wide. You can alter these dimensions to fit your particular blotter holder. Cut this band into three pieces; two which are 23¼ inches long each, and one 12½ inches. Machine stitch the two longer pieces at each end

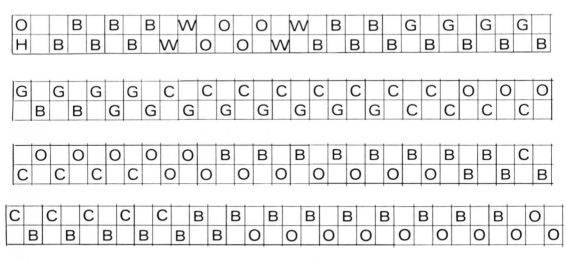

Illus. 26. Threading draft for the desk set in Illus. 25.
Key: B = medium blue, W = white, O = olive, G = grey,
C = coral.

22

Illus. 27. Brush glue onto the side panels of the blotter holder, as well as onto the backs of the two longer inkle pieces.

Illus. 28. Use masking tape to hold the ends of the inkles in place while the glue dries.

to prevent fraying. (You may wish to stitch the pieces before cutting them.) Machine stitch the shorter piece at one end only. Leave a 2-inch fringe free at the other end. You will use this piece to trim the pencil cup (see Illus. 25).

Brush glue onto the side panels of the blotter holder and onto the back of the two longer inkle pieces (see Illus. 27). Carefully press the bands onto the blotter panels one at a time. Turn $\frac{3}{4}$ inch of each band over the ends of the panel and press to the back of the blotter holder. You may use masking tape to hold these ends in place until the glue dries (see Illus. 28).

Cut a piece of poster board to fit the overall size of the blotter holder and glue it to the back of the holder. This covers the inkle ends and gives a finished appearance.

To complete the desk set, make a pencil cup to match the blotter holder. Paint a $15\frac{1}{2}$-ounce can with model enamel. You do not have to paint the area you will cover with the inkle band. When

the paint is dry, brush glue onto the exterior of the can, as well as on the back of the inkle, and press it in place, allowing the fringe to overlap the area where the band meets on the side of the can (see Illus. 29). This completes your desk set—a perfect gift for anyone from a graduate to a grandparent.

Illus. 29. Brush glue onto the outside of a painted tin can to make a pencil cup. Press the inkle in place, as shown, overlapping the fringe where the ends meet.

Clothing Trim

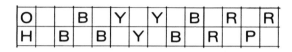

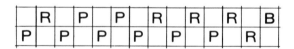

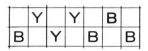

Illus. 31. Threading draft for the trim in Illus. 33. Key: B = medium brown, R = red, Y = yellow, P = pink.

Materials
- inkle loom and shuttle
- 26 heddles
- 2-ply rya (the following colors were used for the trims in Illus. 33: $1\frac{3}{4}$ ounces each of medium brown and red, $1\frac{1}{4}$ ounces each of yellow and pink)
- clothing items to trim
- needle and sewing thread

When you add inkles as trim to clothing, they lend verve and style. See Illus. 33 for two articles decorated with inkles. Bright colors trim the front panel and cuffs of otherwise ordinary shirts and hats. You can also attach inkle bands to the cuffs of your blue jeans. The 2-ply rya yarns are good choices for these inkles and their colors are vibrant and varied.

Weave two inkle strips following the drafts in Illus. 30 and Illus. 31 to make bands like those in Illus. 33. The length of the strips you weave depends on how much trim you need for the article of clothing you have chosen. You can even use short lengths of inkles left over from other projects for trim, where you only need small pieces, such as for the cuffs of a shirt.

Cut the woven inkle band into the desired lengths, machine stitch the ends and press under $\frac{1}{4}$-inch hems. Pin the pieces onto the item you are trimming and then whip them in place with an invisible stitch and a matching sewing thread (see Illus. 34 and 35).

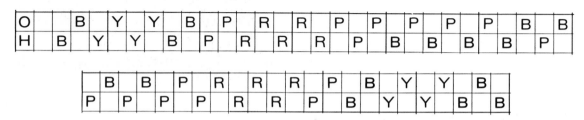

Illus. 30. Threading draft for the trim in Illus. 33. Key: B = medium brown, R = red, Y = yellow, P = pink.

Illus. 32 (right). Even the relatively small pieces of inkle bands used here add a special charm to this solid-colored dress.

Illus. 33 (left). A hat and a jacket—like the ones pictured—are only two articles of clothing which you can decoratively adorn with woven inkle bands.

Illus. 34. First pin the inkle into place on the item of clothing you are decorating, and then sew it securely with an invisible overcast stitch. This is a sleeve of the dress in Illus. 32.

Illus. 35. Pin the trim on the jacket in Illus. 33 as shown here, and then stitch it in place with invisible overcast stitches.

To trim a hat, wrap a 40-inch length of the narrower band with a 1½-inch fringe at each end around the crown of the hat and secure it with half a knot tie (see Illus. 36). Take a few blind stitches with a needle and thread in the tie to fasten it permanently.

Use your imagination to revitalize your wardrobe.

Illus. 36. Trimming a hat is not difficult —and it looks great! Tie a simple half knot, as shown, and secure it in place with a few blind stitches.

Dog Leash

Materials
  inkle loom and shuttle
  17 heddles
  ½ ounce of 10/2 linen (equal amounts of brown, beige and coral were used for the leash in Illus. 39)
  snap shackle
  needle and thread

Tube Weaving

This dog leash introduces a new technique in inkle weaving. You may weave a tube from an inkle band by inserting the shuttle into each shed from the same side of the inkle. Such tubes make excellent handles for handbags or shopping bags and even imaginative wall hangings. You can change from weaving a flat inkle into weaving a tube and then switch back to a flat band all on one warp, as this project demonstrates.

Use a strong thread for your dog's leash; 10/2 linen is a good choice. Warp the loom following

O		B	B	B	G	B	C
H	B	G	G	G	G	B	

	C	C	C	C	C	B	G
B	B	B	B	B	B	G	

	B	B	B	
G	G	G	B	

Illus. 37. Threading draft for the dog leash in Illus. 39. Key: B = brown, G = beige, C = coral.

the draft in Illus. 37, or one you have created. An inkle tube can only be successfully made with a fairly narrow inkle band, so never plan a wide design. A 64-inch warp is sufficient in length.

Do not use cardboard strips to start your weaving as usual. Leave about 4 inches unwoven. Take the first shot through the shed from right to left with your shuttle and pull it quite firmly, closing the warp (see Illus. 38). Bring the shuttle from left

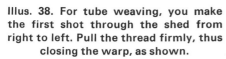

Illus. 38. For tube weaving, you make the first shot through the shed from right to left. Pull the thread firmly, thus closing the warp, as shown.

Illus. 39 (left). Your dog will be the talk of the town with a snappy, hand-made leash such as this one.

Illus. 40. Any guitar player you know would be proud to use a guitar strap like the inkle-woven one shown here. Create an original design from bright colors for an especially attractive strap.

Illus. 41. An eyeglass case is only one of many items you can make using scraps and left-over pieces of inkles. Page 46 has instructions for making this case, as well as ideas for other useful projects using remnant inkles.

Illus. 42 (right). Incorporating beads into your inkle weaving is another creative possibility with this craft. This beaded collar, whose instructions begin on page 44, is fun—and easy—to make.

Illus. 43 (left). Many children have suspenders holding up their clothes. But not too many have as unusual ones as those pictured here. Inkle bands make perfect and cheerful suspenders. Instructions begin on page 39.

Illus. 44. By always weaving from right to left, you create a rounded tube, as shown here.

to right underneath the band, insert it in the alternate shed (again from right to left), and beat it hard. Pass the shuttle on through, pulling the weft very firmly to bring the two selvages of the inkle close together, forming the tube as shown in Illus. 44.

Continue weaving in this way until you are about 8 inches from the end of the warp. At this point, weave in the conventional manner, inserting the shuttle alternately in the left and right sides of the sheds. Your piece will now flatten out into a regular inkle band, as you can see in Illus. 45. Weave this flat section for 3 inches and then cut your piece from the loom.

Illus. 45. To make the dog leash, you tube weave until you are about 8 inches from the end of the warp. Then, you begin to insert the shuttle alternately from the right and left sides, as usual. The tube flattens out again, as you can see.

Illus. 46. Insert the fringed end of the inkle through the metal loop of the snap shackle.

Illus. 47. Forming a 5-inch loop, place the tube into the flat part of the woven band as, shown here.

Purchase a snap shackle for a dog's leash from a hardware store. Insert the 4-inch fringed end through the metal loop at the end of the shackle, as shown in Illus. 46, double the fringe back upon itself, and bind with a 15-inch length of brown linen as shown in Illus. 48.

At the other end of the leash, make a 5-inch loop for the handle. Lay the inkle tube in the flat woven band. (See Illus. 47.) Wrap the tube in the band, whipping the edges together over the tube with a matching sewing thread. Let the fringe hang loose as a decorative touch.

Your dog will surely have his ego boosted by this unique leash.

Illus. 48. To bind the fringe, make a loop with a 15-inch strand of yarn. Wrap the yarn neatly round itself and the fringe you are binding, leaving an inch of yarn at the top. When you have bound the length you want, stick the end of the yarn through the protruding loop and pull the top end, drawing the loop within the bound area. Trim the top end.

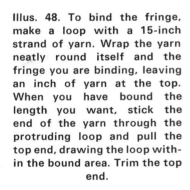
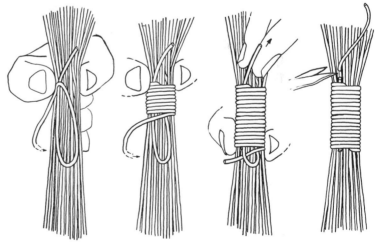

Luggage Rack

Materials
  inkle loom and shuttle
  44 heddles
  2 ounces of 10/2 linen (approximately equal
    amounts of olive, tan, white, lavender and
    rose-lavender were used for the rack in
    Illus. 52)
  carpet tacks
  hammer
  string

A great way to restore an old luggage rack is to replace the worn straps with inkle bands woven to blend with your furnishings. The colors for this project were selected to complement antique furniture and oriental rugs, but you can, of course, choose any colors you want. The material is 10/2 linen, chosen for its strength, firmness and flat finish.

Weave one inkle strip 60 inches long, using the draft in Illus. 49. This gives you a band about $2\frac{1}{4}$ inches wide. Measure three lengths of band, each 18 inches long. Cut them apart and machine stitch each end of the lengths to prevent fraying. (You may prefer to do the stitching on the band first and then cut them apart.)

Before removing the old straps from the rack, tie a string round the bars of the rack to hold it together. Remove the old straps and replace them with the new ones, using either carpet tacks, as shown in Illus. 50, or a heavy-duty stapler, as shown in Illus. 51. This quick and easy job results in a handsome good-as-new luggage rack, like the one in Illus. 52.

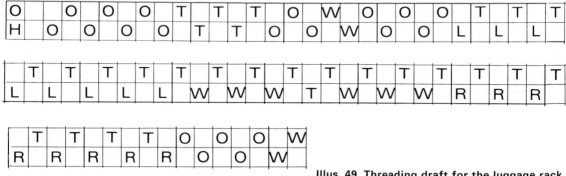

Illus. 49. Threading draft for the luggage rack in Illus. 52. Key: O = olive, T = tan, W = white, L = lavender, R = rose lavender.

Illus. 50. You can attach your newly woven straps to a wooden luggage rack frame with carpet tacks, as shown here.

Illus. 52. A luggage rack is a unique item in any bedroom or guest room. If you have one, you can make it even more outstanding if you replace worn-out straps with new ones you weave on your inkle loom.

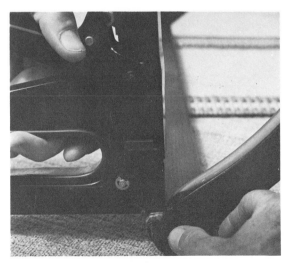

Illus. 51. Or, you can attach the woven straps to the frame with a heavy-duty stapler, as shown here.

Illus. 53. Always looking for new ideas for pillows? Inkle trim is ideal! See the next page for the instructions for this lovely pillow.

Pillow Trim

Materials
    inkle loom and shuttle
    27 heddles
    4 ounces of 2-ply rya yarn (equal parts of navy,
        periwinkle, deep rose, medium rose, white
        and red were used for the pillow in Illus. 53)
    14-inch × 14-inch polyester pillow form
    ½ yard fabric remnant
    needle and sewing thread

Illus. 55. To trim a pillow like the one shown in Illus. 53, fold your completed inkle as shown here.

You can make attractive couch pillows by attaching inkle bands to pillow forms that you cover with remnants of fabric. Visit your local upholstery shop and pick up inexpensive pieces of antique velvet or other handsome fabrics and stitch a pillow cover. Then cut your inkle to whatever length you desire to fit on the pillow top. Illus. 53 suggests one way you can sew inkles onto a pillow using an invisible whipping stitch.

To make a band like the one in Illus. 53, use 2-ply rya yarn to weave a 72-inch inkle following the draft in Illus. 54. Cut the band into four pieces each 18 inches long, including a 1½-inch fringe at the ends. Fold each piece so that you form a point as shown in Illus. 55. Lay these four sections on

O		M	N	N	N	P	P	P	P	R	R	P	P	W		D
H		M	N	N	N	P	P	P	P	P	R	R	P	P	W	

		D		D		D		D		M		M		M		M		M		M		M		M
	D		D		M		M		M		W		W		W		W		W		W		W		M

Illus. 54. Threading draft for the pillow trim in Illus. 53. Key: N = navy, P = periwinkle, D = deep rose, M = medium rose, W = white, R = red.

Illus. 56. Lay the four folded sections of trim on the pillow top as shown. Pin them in place and then sew them securely.

the pillow top so that the points of each meet at the middle of the pillow as shown in Illus. 56. Pin the bands in place and whip all edges to the pillow. Leave the fringe hanging free.

You can devise your own way to fold and attach inkle bands to a pillow. Mix a plain band with one of an intricate pattern to cover the entire top if you wish.

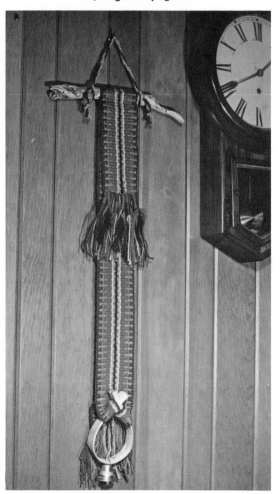

Illus. 57 (left). If you are a true plant lover, you will surely want your plants to have as pretty a hanger as the one shown here. Instructions for this wooden and woven plant hanger (you need only basic carpentry and weaving skills to make it) begin on page 41.

Illus. 58 (right). A bell pull is often just the right thing to fill up an empty space on a wall. See the next page for the instructions for this bell pull, which incorporates a hand-carved, Greek goat bell for special interest.

Bell Pull

Materials
   inkle loom and shuttle
   36 heddles
   4 ounces of 2-ply rya yarn (equal amounts brown, brick red and grey-beige and small amounts white, medium grey, light grey and dark grey were used for the bell pull in Illus. 58)
   piece of driftwood, branch or dowel
   a small bell and collar
   feathers
   needle and sewing thread

Inkles make excellent bell pulls which you can use as decorative wall hangings. You may weave and finish them in a variety of ways. You can purchase bells at craft shops or museums. Camel bells are frequently available. The unique bell used in Illus. 58 is a hand-carved, Greek goat bell on a goat collar. (See suppliers list on page 47.)

You need a warp approximately 65 inches long for this project. Using 2-ply rya yarn, warp your loom following the draft in Illus. 59. Begin weaving 7 inches from dowel #1, thus allowing for fringe.

Use the brown for the weft and fill two shuttles. Find the middle of the warp and weave in two sections starting with one shuttle on the right. Put it through the shed to the middle, change sheds and beat. Take the second shuttle and, starting at the middle, put it through the second, left-hand section of the warp. Change sheds and beat. (See Illus. 60.) Place the beginning ends in each section in the usual manner.

Continue weaving first on the right side with the right shuttle and then on the left side with the left shuttle, changing sheds in the usual way until the two parallel sections measure 5 inches in length.

Now pull the two sections together by putting both shuttles through each shed about three times as you weave in the normal fashion (see Illus. 61). Then cut one of the wefts, ending it by wrapping

O		B	B	B	B	B	G	R	R	R	R	R	R	R	R
H	B	B	G	G	G	G	G	G	G	G	R	R	R	R	

	W	L	M	D	M	L	W	R	R	R	R	R	R	R	R
W	L	M	D	D	M	L	W	R	R	R	R	G	G	G	

	G	B	B	B	B	B
G	G	G	G	G	B	B

Illus. 59. Threading draft for the bell pull in Illus. 58. Key: B = brown, R = brick red, G = grey-beige, W = white, M = medium grey, L = light grey, D = dark grey.

Illus. 60. To create the split in the bell pull shown in Illus. 58, weave the left- and right-hand sections separately, as shown.

Illus. 61. To pull the sections together, weave through both sections with both shuttles.

Illus. 62. To finish the bell pull, wrap the split sections around each side of the clasp of the goat collar, as shown.

it round the end selvage warp and placing it in the same shed you have just woven. Finish weaving the length of the inkle using just one shuttle. Leave 6 inches of unwoven warp at the end for the fringe. Cut the inkle from the loom.

To finish your bell pull like the one in Illus. 58, wrap the narrow, split sections around each side of the clasp of the goat collar. Tack them with sewing thread to the whole inkle, as shown in Illus. 62. Then let the fringed end hang down behind the collar and bell.

Loop the top of the bell pull over a piece of driftwood or dowel, letting the other fringed end hang over in front about one-third of the way down. Tack it in place near the dowel.

The top fringe in Illus. 58 was bound with two colors—bright red and maroon. A few feathers were bound in with some of the fringe. See Illus. 48 for binding instructions.

To hang the bell pull, attach a twisted cord, made from some lengths of the yarn, to both sides of the driftwood or dowel. Instructions for making a twist are on pages 19-20.

Suspenders

Materials

inkle loom and shuttle

30 heddles

$1\frac{3}{4}$ ounces of 10/2 linen ($\frac{3}{4}$ ounce white and light blue, $\frac{1}{4}$ ounce red were used for the suspenders in Illus. 43)

suspender grippers

needle and sewing thread

Pick-up Technique

One of the most interesting variations in inkle weaving, the pick-up technique, allows for endless design possibilities. It is a finger-manipulated process whereby you temporarily lift selected warps with your fingers to weave them with the opposite shed. The pick-up technique is characteristic of native Americans, particularly those from Guatemala, Bolivia and the southwest United States. Black and white or natural are frequently used for the pattern and background, while narrow stripes of white and red or green form the border. The patterns are geometric, usually with diagonal or horizontal configurations. You may work a pattern out first on graph paper, or simply begin designing on the loom as you weave.

A 10/2 linen was chosen for the child's suspenders shown in Illus. 43, for it is strong and does not stretch. A 5-foot inkle is a sufficient length for a pair of suspenders for a five-year-old-child like the one shown in Illus. 43. Follow the draft in Illus. 63 to warp your loom.

You do not need a fringe, so begin your weaving as close to dowel #1 as possible. Start by lifting the warp with your left hand. Since you warp the white threads in the open (between heddles), this raises all the white warp in the design area. Put the shuttle through from left to right. Next depress the warp (all the blue threads are now up) and weave from right to left. Weave seven plain rows in this manner.

On the eighth row, you are ready to do your first pick-up. Follow the graph pattern in Illus. 64, reading from the bottom to top. Insert your left hand in the shed (which is down) and start at the right edge, picking up the desired warps with your right hand—in this case, threads 4, 6, 8, 10, 12, 14, 16 of the white warp. Lift these with your

O		W	R	W	R	R	W	W	W	W	W	W	W	W
H	W	R	W	W	R	R	B	B	B	B	B	B	B	B

					W	W	W	W	W	W	W	W
				B	B	B	B	B	B	B	B

			W	W	R	R	W	R	W
		B	B	R	R	W	W	R	W

Illus. 63. Threading draft for the suspenders in Illus. 43. Key: W = white, B = light blue, R = red.

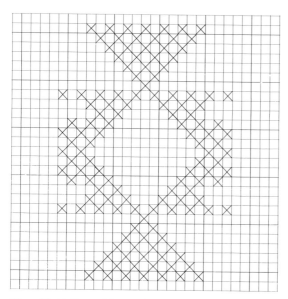

Illus. 64. Follow this graph to duplicate the pick-up pattern in the suspenders in Illus. 43.

right hand and hold them along with those warp threads raised in making this shed (see Illus. 65). Pass the shuttle through, change the shed and beat in the usual manner. Weave from left to right with a plain row (see Illus. 66).

The warps that you raised with your fingers form a float (not tied down by the weft) over three wefts. You cannot raise them again by hand until you have tied them down by weaving them in a regular row.

On the next pass of the weft from right to left, raise alternate warp threads—in this case, threads 5, 7, 9, 11, 13, 15. As you pass your right hand from one pattern warp to pick up to the next, note that you go under two threads in the warp that is raised, blue threads in this instance. This helps you to find the correct white threads to pick up from the warp that is down.

Follow the graph until you have finished one pattern. Then weave five rows plain and begin again at the bottom of the graph, repeating the pattern. Continue in this manner for the length of the inkle. Remove the band from the loom and cut it in two near the middle, but at the beginning of a new pattern. Machine stitch all ends to prevent fraying.

Buy hardware for the suspenders at a fabric

Illus. 65. The pick-up technique involves picking up certain threads from the shed that is down, and then incorporating them with the raised shed.

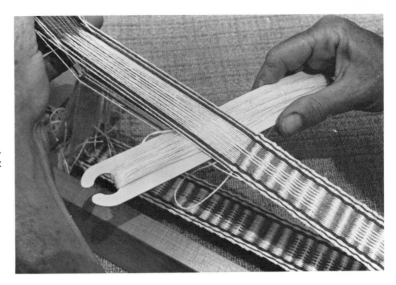

Illus. 66. After a pick-up row, you weave from left to right with a plain row.

shop or notions counter. Slip the inkle bands through the slots of the suspender clips according to the directions that accompany the clips or grippers. Cross the suspenders in the back and sew them to the top of the pants or skirt. Attach the grippers to the front.

Try making your own pick-up patterns after you have mastered the technique.

Plant Hanger

Materials
    inkle loom and two shuttles
    22 heddles
    2 ounces of 10/2 linen (equal amounts of gold, coral and beige were used for the plant hanger in Illus. 57)
    driftwood or dowel
    10 feet of parting strips ($\frac{3}{4}$ inch $\times$ $\frac{1}{2}$ inch)

    $\frac{1}{2}$ pint stain
    30 one-inch brads

To make an attractive plant hanger like the one in Illus. 57, you need to sharpen your carpentry skills as well as your weaving ones. The techniques and skills you need are elementary, however, so do not despair.

To make a platform for the planter, purchase 10 feet of $\frac{3}{4}$ inch $\times$ $\frac{1}{2}$ inch parting strips at a lumber yard (these are not expensive). Cut this

41

O		G	G	G	G	G	G	G	G	G	C	C	G	G	G
H	G	G	C	C	C	C	C	C	C	C	C	G	G	B	

	G	G	G	G	G	G	G
B	B	B	B	B	B	G	G

Illus. 67. Threading draft for the plant hanger in Illus. 57. Key: C = coral, G = gold, B = beige.

into nine lengths of $12\frac{3}{4}$ inches each. Lay five pieces out parallel to each other with $1\frac{1}{2}$-inch gaps between the pieces. With 1-inch brads, nail two pieces across these five strips, leaving a $1\frac{1}{2}$-inch overhang on all outside ends (see Illus. 70). Now nail the remaining two strips across the ends of these two latter strips. Stain the finished platform.

Now to the weaving. Follow the threading draft in Illus. 67, using 10/2 linen. Leave 4 inches for fringe and weave for $1\frac{1}{2}$ inches in the usual fashion. Next, you need to weave a slit in the middle of the inkle band, so you must wind an

Illus. 68. To make a slit, you weave with two shuttles—first to the middle of the band with one and all the way across with the other, and then halfway across with each.

additional shuttle with the same color weft as your first. Start weaving with this shuttle along with the first shuttle for three or four shots before you weave the slit. This lends extra strength and prevents fraying at the point of the slit. Your band should measure exactly 2 inches when you begin to weave the slit (exclusive of fringe).

Weave to the middle of the band with one shuttle and all the way across with the second shuttle. Change sheds and beat. Now weave just halfway across the band with each shuttle—from the middle to the selvage with the first shuttle and from the selvage to the middle with the second one (see Illus. 68). Change sheds and beat.

Continue weaving in this way until the slit measures $1\frac{1}{4}$ inches. Close the slit by again weaving all the way across the band at least three shots with both shuttles (see Illus. 69). Cut the extra weft free and end it in the usual fashion. Weave for 31 inches with the first shuttle. Now weave another slit, $1\frac{1}{4}$ inches long, just as you wove the first slit. Close the slit in the same way and weave a total of 2 inches. Plan a 4-inch fringe at this end also.

You need to weave four such pieces for your plant hanger. If you weave two on one warp, be sure to leave 8 inches between the woven areas for a 4-inch fringe on each end. If you make sure you locate the slits at the same place on each band

Illus. 69. To close the slit, weave all the way across at least three times with both shuttles.

Illus. 70. Attach the woven bands at the four corners as shown.

it will be easier to hang a level platform for your plant.

Cut the bands apart and trim the fringe. Pass the end of one band under a corner of the frame, pulling it up inside. Pull the free end of the band through the slit at this corner as shown in Illus. 70. Attach the other three bands to the corners of the frame similarly.

To hang the project on your driftwood or dowel, you need to form a loop at the free end of each band where you have woven a second slit. Begin by pulling the fringed end through the slit as in Illus. 71. Keep pulling this end through the slit, curling the edges of the slit as shown in Illus. 72. Stuff the edges through the slit until you are pulling the continuous part of the band through the slit to form a loop that you can adjust to fit the driftwood or dowel.

Slip the loops onto the dowel and adjust them snugly. Make a twist of some of the linen, following the directions on pages 19–20. Attach each end of the twist to the dowel or driftwood for hanging. Hang this project indoors or outside.

Illus. 71. To attach the bands to the dowel or driftwood, first make a loop at the top, where you made a slit in the band.

Illus. 72. Then, continue to pull the end through the slit, curling the edges as shown, until you create a loop from the continuous part of the inkle. Slip this loop onto the dowel or driftwood.

Beaded Collar

Illus. 74. Slip beads onto some of the open warp threads as you warp the loom for this project.

Materials

inkle loom and shuttle

33 heddles

3 ounces of 2-ply rya yarn (1-ounce medium lime, $\frac{1}{2}$ ounce each white, pale lime, coral and French blue were used for the collar in Illus. 42)

26 glass beads of assorted colors to blend with the yarn

When you incorporate beads in an inkle-woven piece, they add charm and sophistication to your weaving. Choose beads that have large enough holes to slip easily onto the warp, but the beads themselves should not be so large that they throw the weft shots too far out of alignment as you weave. Glass beads from India were used for the collar in Illus. 42.

Warp the loom following the draft in Illus. 73, but as you do so, slip beads at random onto some of the open warp threads across the width of the warp (see Illus. 74). Do not put beads on heddle warp threads. As you progress, push the beads on the warp ahead of your weaving. Occasionally slip one or more beads against the web before you change the shed. Then change the shed and lock the bead into place. The beads in the collar shown in Illus. 42 are concentrated at the front of the collar, but they need not be (see Illus. 75).

O		L		L		P		L		L		W		B		B		B		W		C		C		C		C
H		L		L		P		L		L		W	W		B		B		W		L		L		L		L

	C		C		C		C		C		C		L		W		B		W		P		P		P		L		P
L		L		L		L		L		L		L		W		B		W		P		P		P		P		L

	P		L		L
P		P		L		L

Illus. 73. Threading draft for the beaded collar in Illus. 42. Key: L = medium lime, W = white, P = pale lime, C = coral, B = blue.

Illus. 75. Before you change the shed, move one or more beads against the woven web. When you change the shed, you lock the bead or beads in place.

This collar is woven in segments To do this, weave the middle section (warp threads 8 to 50, counting from the left side of the draft) for $1\frac{1}{2}$ inches. Then weave across threads 1 to 50 for 2 inches more. Use cardboard strips for each new segment you add to help anchor the weft in place (see Illus. 76). Finally, weave across the entire width of the warp (threads 1 to 66).

When this section, across the width of the warp, measures 4 inches in length, begin weaving a slit by using two shuttles following the directions for the hanging planter on page 42. The slit should measure $11\frac{1}{2}$ inches. Then, re-join the two halves of warp, weaving with the weft from both shuttles for at least three shots to reinforce the end of the slit. Discontinue one weft and weave 2 inches from the slit. Leave $4\frac{1}{2}$ inches of unwoven warp for fringe.

You can finish weaving any warp left on the loom. Use this woven remnant later for many small projects (see page 46 for instructions).

The fringe at both the front and the back of the collar in Illus. 42 were plied for a further decora-tive effect. To ply two ends, first twist one thread to the right until it kinks. Hold it with a pinch clothespin while you twist the second thread tightly to the right also. Then put the two ends together, stretching them out and twisting them both to the left until they are well plied. Knot the ends and trim them.

Your collar is ready to wear.

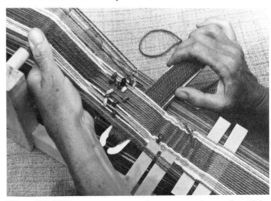

Illus. 76. When you weave in segments, as for this collar, use cardboard strips, as shown, to help anchor the weft in place for each new section.

Eyeglass Case

Materials
    inkle remnants of any material (17¾-inch length)
    needle and sewing thread

Often, when you weave an inkle band for a project, you have a short length left over. Save these odds and ends and use them to make such small items as coin purses, pin cushions, coasters, book marks, sachets or eyeglass cases. Inkles made of any materials are suitable for them.

To make an eyeglass case, cut a piece of inkle to

a 17¾-inch length. The width of inkle you need for this project depends on the style of glasses. A wide inkle, about 3½ inches, is best for glasses with heavy, plastic frames while a 2¾-inch width will do for wire-frame glasses. A narrower inkle, 2½ inches wide, will suffice for most styles of half-glasses.

If the band does not already have a fringed end, make a 2-inch fringe by pulling out the weft. Machine stitch the opposite woven end and turn under a ½-inch hem. Steam press and whip it in place by hand.

Now measure 6¾ inches from this edge and fold the band in half with the hemmed edge inside. Fold the fringed edge back to the outside so that the fold lays directly on top of the hemmed edge (see Illus. 77). Pin the long side edges together and then whip them with a matching sewing thread. The fringe falls free on the top of your glasses case as a decoration.

Small items such as this eyeglass case are quick and easy to make and are perfect to sell at a bazaar or craft fair, or simply to give as gifts. See what other things you can create from your left-over inkles.

Illus. 77. Fold a remnant piece of inkle as shown to make an eyeglass case like the one shown in Illus. 41.

Suppliers

Inkle Looms

Dick Blick
P.O. Box 1267
Galesburg, Illinois 61401

Lily Mills Company
P.O. Box 88
Shelby, North Carolina 28150
(also cotton yarn)

Morgan Inkle Loom Factory
Railroad Engine House
Guilford, Connecticut 06437

School Products
1201 Broadway
New York, New York 10001
(also 2-ply Cum Asbo Rya yarn)

Schacht Spindle Co.
1708 Walnut Street
Boulder, Colorado 80302

Tahki Imports Ltd.
336 West End Avenue
New York, New York 10023
(also Greek goat bell)

Yarns

Briggs & Little's Woolen Mill Ltd.
York Mills, Harvey Station, P.O.
York County
New Brunswick, Canada
  (2/8 100 per cent wool yarn)

Craftsman's Mark Yarns
Trefnant, Denbigh
North Wales, U.K.
  2/5's Floor rug yarn (natural shades)

Fort Crailo Yarns Co.
2 Green Street
Rensselaer, New York 12144
  (2-ply Crailo Rya)

Frederick J. Fawcett Incorporated
129 South Street
Boston, Massachusetts 02111
  (10/2 linen)

J. Hyslop Bathgate & Co.
Galashiels TD1 1NY
Scotland
  (2/2½'s Worsted Tapestry)

William Condon & Sons
P.O. Box 129
Charlottetown
Prince Edward Island, Canada
  (2-ply wool yarn and beads)

Index